Animal Classification

Birds

by Erica Donner

Bullfrog Books

Ideas for Parents and Teachers

Bullfrog Books let children practice reading informational text at the earliest reading levels. Repetition, familiar words, and photo labels support early readers.

Before Reading

- Discuss the cover photo. What does it tell them?

- Look at the picture glossary together. Read and discuss the words.

Read the Book

- "Walk" through the book and look at the photos. Let the child ask questions. Point out the photo labels.

- Read the book to the child, or have him or her read independently.

After Reading

- Prompt the child to think more. Ask: What different kinds of birds have you seen before?

Bullfrog Books are published by Jump!
5357 Penn Avenue South
Minneapolis, MN 55419
www.jumplibrary.com

Library of Congress Cataloging-in-Publication Data

Names: Donner, Erica, author.
Title: Birds / by Erica Donner.
Description: Minneapolis, MN : Jump! Inc., [2017]
Series: Animal classification | Audience: Ages 5-8.
Audience: K to grade 3. | Includes bibliographical references and index.
Identifiers: LCCN 2016030214 (print)
LCCN 2016039163 (ebook)
ISBN 9781620315378 (hard cover: alk. paper)
ISBN 9781620315910 (pbk.)
ISBN 9781624964800 (e-book)
Subjects: LCSH: Birds—Juvenile literature.
Classification: LCC QL676.2 .F73 2017 (print)
LCC QL676.2 (ebook) | DDC 598—dc23
LC record available at https://lccn.loc.gov/2016030214

Editor: Kirsten Chang
Book Designer: Molly Ballanger
Photo Researcher: Kirsten Chang

Photo Credits: All photos by Shutterstock except:
Alamy, 17; iStock, 15; Superstock, 6–7, 10–11, 18, 23tl, 23bl; Thinkstock, 1.

Printed in the United States of America at Corporate Graphics in North Mankato, Minnesota.

Table of Contents

Feathered Fliers

Look up!

What do you see?

Ducks!
A duck is a
kind of bird.

5

wings

What makes a bird?

Birds have feathers.

Feathers cover
a bird's body.

They cover their wings.

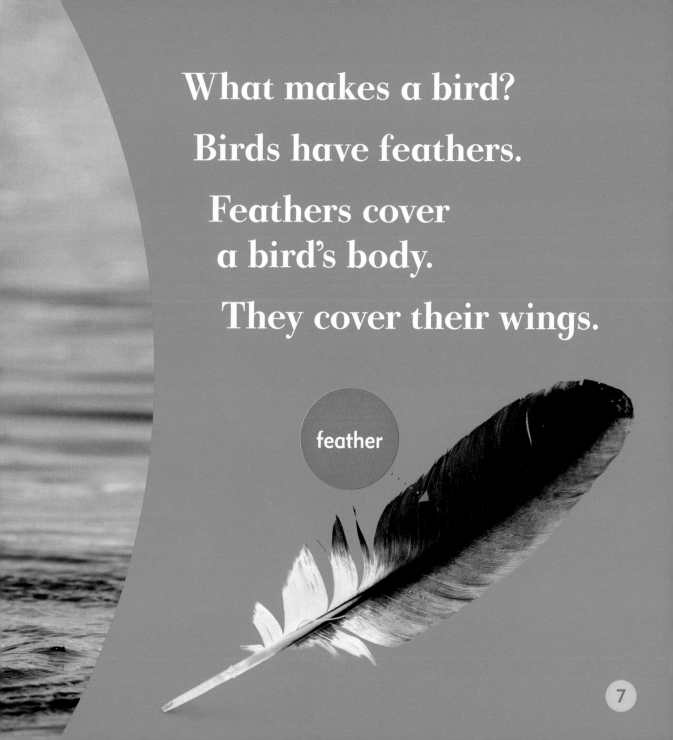

feather

All birds have wings.

Most birds use
them to fly.

ostrich

But not all birds fly.

Penguins can swim.

Ostriches can run.

But neither can fly.

Birds are warm-blooded.

They can make their own heat.

This lets them live in cold places.

penguin

13

Birds lay eggs.
Soon these
eggs will hatch.

eggs

14

Look! Robins!

Mama feeds them.

She uses her beak.

beak

All birds have beaks.

Beaks crack seeds.

They peck for insects.

Birds come in all sizes.
Some birds are huge.
A condor is a bird.

18

**Some birds are tiny.
A hummingbird
is a bird, too.**

Birds are cool!

What Makes a Bird?

beak
Birds use their beaks for eating, grooming, fighting, courting, and feeding young.

wings
All birds have wings, but not all birds use them to fly; penguins use theirs as flippers to swim.

feathers
A bird's feathers are important for flight, insulation, and waterproofing.

bones
A bird's bones are hollow; this makes them lighter, making it easier to get off the ground.

Picture Glossary

condor
A large South American bird of prey.

penguin
An aquatic, flightless bird; many penguins live in Antarctica.

ostrich
A large, flightless bird of Africa; ostriches are the heaviest of all birds.

warm-blooded
Able to maintain a constant body temperature regardless of environment.

Index

To Learn More

Learning more is as easy as 1, 2, 3.

1) Go to www.factsurfer.com

2) Enter "birds" into the search box.

3) Click the "Surf" button to see a list of websites.

With factsurfer.com, finding more information is just a click away.